We Need to Go to School

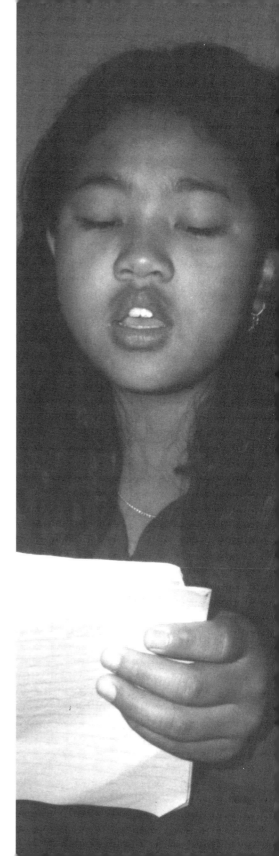

We acknowledge the financial support of the
Canada Council for the Arts, the Ontario Arts
Council and the Government of Canada
 through the Book
Publishing Industry
Development Program for
our publishing activities.

ONTARIO ARTS COUNCIL
CONSEIL DES ARTS DE L'ONTARIO

Groundwood Books / Douglas & McIntyre
720 Bathurst Street, Suite 500
Toronto, Ontario M5S 2R4
Distributed in the USA by
Publishers Group West
1700 Fourth Street, Berkeley, CA 94710

National Library of Canada
Cataloguing in Publication Data
Main entry under title:
We need to go to school: voices of the
Rugmark children
"A Groundwood book".
ISBN 0-88899-425-7 (bound) ISBN 0-88899-
426-5 (pbk.)
1. Child labor – Nepal – Juvenile literature. 2.
Rug and carpet industry – Nepal – Employees
– Juvenile literature. 3. Rugmark (Association)
– Juvenile literature. 4. Children's writings,
Nepali. I. Roberts-Davis, Tanya, 1982- .
HD6247.R942N47 2001   j331.3'1'095496
C00-932503-4

Printed and bound in Canada by union labor

A Groundwood Book
Douglas & McIntyre
Toronto Vancouver Buffalo

To all children, whose power to change the world for
the better cannot be underestimated.

Acknowledgments

The process of compiling this book could never have been suc-
cessful without the support, input and facilitation of many dedicated people, all of whom deserve my gratitude. I would like to
thank the staff at Groundwood Books, in particular Patsy
Aldana, Michael Solomon and editor Shelley Tanaka, for their
patience, determination and much-needed expertise. I am also
grateful to *Toronto Star* columnist Michele Landsberg for writing a
supportive article about my work in Nepal, widening the possi-
bility of publishing the stories of the Rugmark children. Cathy
Cameron, former executive director of Rugmark Canada, helped
to develop the idea for this book and has been continuously supportive as well as encouraging.

I extend my sincere appreciation to the staff at Danforth
Collegiate for their unfailing support, encouragement and flexi-
bility. Generous financial assistance was provided by them as well
as by the Canadian Auto Workers' Social Justice Fund, the
Steelworkers' Humanities Fund, Rugmark Canada and the
Union of Needletrades, Industrial and Textile Employees. Several
family members read through the text and contributed helpful
advice, including my mother, Dale Roberts, my younger brother
Ivan, my grandmother Dorothy Roberts and my uncle Wayne
Roberts. All offered strength, insight, laughter and love.

Caroline Bakker has been an understanding and warm-heart-
ed friend who welcomed me with open arms in Kathmandu.
Dedicated and patient, Namrata Sharma provided the much-
needed translations during my discussions with the students and
teachers of the Rugmark schools. The staff of Rugmark Nepal,
particularly Saroj Rai, Kumar Pandey and Shrada Shrestha, pre-
sented me with insights into the Nepali carpet industry and cul-
ture by taking me to factories, villages and schools. With the aid
of the teachers of the Rugmark schools, the times during which I
worked with the students proceeded smoothly.

Selflessly drawing me into their lives, the children at the
Rugmark schools never ceased to amaze me with their enthusiasm, compassion and optimism. By openly sharing their
thoughts, experiences and feelings with me, the children made
me realize how important it was for their voices to be heard and,
ultimately, made this book possible.

We Need to Go to School

VOICES OF
THE RUGMARK CHILDREN

COMPILED BY **TANYA ROBERTS–DAVIS**

DOUGLAS & McINTYRE
TORONTO
VANCOUVER
BUFFALO

A GROUNDWOOD BOOK

Childhood Matters

Imagine waking up at five o'clock every morning to start work in a dimly lit carpet factory. Sitting on a hard wooden bench in front of a loom, your job is to quickly tie wool in tiny knots that you then tighten using a heavy toothed hammer. The only windows in the building are small and placed near the ceiling. There are bars across them. At times, you can hear the laughter of school children outside.

You continue to weave until nine o'clock at night. You have only two short meal breaks. A cup of tea and sometimes a small bowl of rice with lentil soup will be given to you as your payment for the day. There is time for just one trip to the toilet. The air is thick with dust from the wool, which gets into your lungs, making your chest ache when you breathe.

This life is real for more than one million children in countries such as Nepal, India and Pakistan. Every day we walk on carpets that could have been made by children who are forced to work in order to help support their families and to survive. Children are employed in these factories because adults demand a better salary, while young workers can be paid little or nothing at all. These children may also be intimidated through regular beatings and sexual assault. They do not have the choice to attend school because it is too expensive. Growing up illiterate and unhealthy, these children

Children at a Rugmark center dramatize weaving a carpet.

and the generation that follows them continue to exist in a vicious cycle of poverty.

Certain kinds of work can have a positive impact on children's development. Young people who help out in a family shop, deliver newspapers or work in the local fields for part of the day can help their families and become more responsible and mature. However, youngsters who toil long hours in unsafe or unhealthy conditions, who are undernourished, who have no time to play or go to school, or who are physically abused are being exploited. They are being denied the rights guaranteed to them in the United Nations Convention on the Rights of the Child.

Exploitative child labor is a complex problem, but part of the solution is to provide all children with the opportunity to go to school, where they can learn to read, become informed about their rights and find the means to escape the stranglehold of poverty.

Through an organization called Rugmark, some child carpet weavers are being given the chance to change their lives. Rugmark labels carpets from Nepal, India and Pakistan to certify that they have been made by adults who are paid a decent wage. Some financial support is provided by UNICEF. Factory owners are allowed to put the Rugmark label on their carpets when they agree to follow strict labor standards. Each factory is then inspected on a regular and surprise basis to ensure that nobody under the age of fourteen is working there and that employees are paid at least the minimum local wage. Any child found working in the factory is invited to

attend a center for education and rehabilitation set up by Rugmark and maintained by a local community group. Students can stay at this school until they are eighteen and have been trained for a job of their choice or, after spending some time at a Rugmark center, they may decide to return to their families and attend a local school, with the education fees paid by Rugmark. Meanwhile, a relative who is unemployed will be encouraged to fill the vacancy at the factory. This policy means that the income stays within the same family.

When I was twelve, I became involved in the youth organization Free the Children, which focuses on the problems of child labor and on empowering young people to make a difference in the world. One of my main tasks was to speak about child exploitation in the workplace at conferences in Canada, Cuba, Germany, Nepal

Education, Protection
and Help for Children –
a Rugmark center.

and the United States. With other young people, I helped
Canadian trade unions and human rights groups to initiate the
founding of Rugmark Canada.

In May, 1999, when I was sixteen, I traveled alone to Nepal
through the generous funding of Canadian trade unions as well as
Rugmark Canada. For six weeks I lived with children in the
Rugmark rehabilitation centers. The purpose of my trip was to
begin to understand the experiences and aspirations of former carpet weavers by hearing what they had to say about their lives and
talking to them directly. A seventeen-year-old Nepalese student
named Namrata Sharma, who spoke English fluently, acted as a
translator.

The four Rugmark centers are the Bal Adhayan thatha Bikas
Kendra (BABK or Hamro Ghar), the Co-operative Society of
Bungmati, the Gyanpunj Service Center, and Education, Protection
and Help for Children. The children in these schools range in age
from nine to sixteen. They called me Didi, which means Older
Sister. Their classrooms sometimes had blackboards that needed
painting and were short of desks, benches, chalk and books. Yet the
children's smiles were contagious and their enthusiasm filled the
whole school. They invented dance routines, had singing contests
and played table tennis on a slab of wood using a line of bricks for
a net. Their desire to learn was truly inspiring to me. Lessons were
mostly calm and serious, involving memorization, but the classrooms would also erupt with frequent giggling. From the moments

An emotional farewell to Tanya at the Co-operative Society of Bungmati.

of shared laughter to the serious times of the interviews, the students taught me about compassion, courage and happiness. They helped me to understand that life may not be perfect, but everyone can be a part of changing the future for the better.

To teach me about their experiences in their villages, carpet factories and at school, the children performed plays that were sometimes so detailed, they lasted for an hour. The students also drew pictures, gave oral accounts and wrote songs, poetry as well as personal stories. At one of the rehabilitation centers, they organized a children's festival to share their perspectives on working in carpet factories and the advantages of attending school. A large crowd came to enjoy the puppet show, poetry reading, a drama, dances, songs and refreshments.

This book is the result of the time I spent in Nepal. Through their own words and pictures, children who worked in the carpet industry present their past and present experiences, as well as their hopes for the future. They may share a common past but, like us, they each have their own fears, accomplishments and dreams. Through their voices we can understand the sense of hope that emerges when children have the opportunity to go to school.

Life in Nepal

Nepal is a small country of great physical beauty, with lush jungles, forested valleys and snow-capped mountains. But it is also one of the poorest countries in the world. Though the tourism industry and the export of hand-woven carpets, textiles, as well as some agricultural products bring much-needed income into the country, more than half the population lives on less than a dollar a day.

The Reality of Poverty in Nepal

Officially, Nepal is a Hindu country. One of the principles of the Hindu religion is the caste system, which determines a person's rank in society and their expectations of life. This system was originally based on professions that were inherited, but today it gives people of the higher castes power over those of a lower status. Individuals of higher castes have easier access to good farm land and better schools, while those belonging to the lowest caste (Untouchables) often cannot use temples, funeral places, public washrooms and drinking taps because they are thought to contaminate all that they touch.

In Nepal, a small number of people own a large portion of the land, and a growing number have no land or insufficient land to grow enough food to live on. There are now 600,000 squatters, or people who have no land and no proper shelter, and many have developed their own makeshift settlements where illiteracy, family violence and drug abuse are widespread. More than seventy percent of the people live in absolute poverty. This means they cannot

- The climate in Nepal is one of extremes. The dry season takes place from October to May, and the wet season of the monsoons occurs between June and September. During December and January, the temperature can fall to -18 C (0 F); during the hottest months of May and June, the temperature can rise to 44 C (110 F).

- Nepal's written history dates back to the seventh century, when the region was divided into small municipalities mainly ruled by wealthy families. Since then the country's political history has been troubled and unstable. Free and democratic elections were not held until 1991.

- Ethnically, Nepal is composed of people who have migrated from Mongolia, India and Tibet. Although the country's 20 million citizens speak a wide variety of tongues, the standard language is Nepali.

A traditional home in the foothills of the Himalayas.

afford the minimum nutritional requirements and are unable to pay for essential non-food requirements such as a shelter. Only thirty-seven percent of the population has access to clean drinking water. About 75,000 children die every year, including 45,000 youngsters under the age of five who die of diarrhea. There are not enough doctors or hospitals, and the average life expectancy is fifty-six years. (In contrast, life expectancy in North America is seventy-eight years.)

Many families work in agriculture for three to eight months of the year and then move to the cities, particularly Kathmandu, to find work for the rest of the year. This movement of people has caused the growth of informal industries that employ the migrants in abusive working conditions, encourage them to take out loans with high rates of interest and draw children as well as adults into debt bondage. One million children work in exploitative conditions in carpet factories, brick kilns, domestic service, agriculture, stone quarries and mines, transportation, on construction sites and in many other dangerous industries. As well, five thousand children live and work

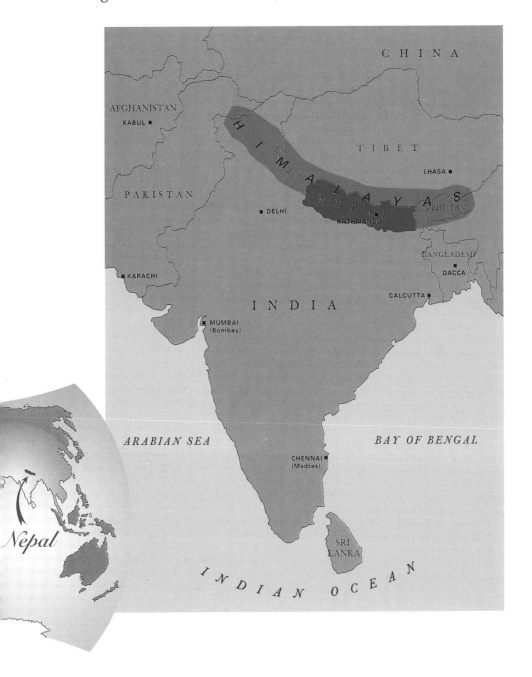

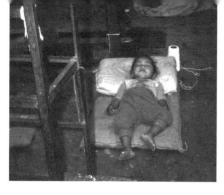

Children of carpet weavers sleep and play in the factories, because there are no daycares.

in the street. (Even though Nepal has ratified the United Nations Convention on the Rights of the Child, has a constitution and has employment standards, the laws are not effectively implemented.)

Education and Girls' Lost Opportunities

Since 1975, free textbooks and tuition have been provided for children in grades one to three. But parents still have to pay for paper, pencils and uniforms, and many cannot afford these expenses. Schools are not always within walking distance of every village, and public transportation is not usually available. Only half the children who enter school complete their primary education.

Because families are so poor, they often want their children to contribute to the family income. Parents have on average five children. Girls, in particular, are seen as a household asset, and an education for them is often considered a waste of money. On average, 39 percent of children enrolled at primary school are girls, and 61 percent are boys. There are also very few women teachers.

In a rural family, a boy is expected to work about three hours a day once he is six years old and five to six hours a day once he turns ten. A girl is expected to work twice as many hours. By age five, many girls in rural settings fetch water, fuel and fodder, tend to the animals, cook, wash clothes and look after younger siblings. Such a work load makes it difficult for them to go to school. By the time they are fifteen, one-third of girls are married and ten percent

Studying together in the girls' dorm of the Co-operative Society of Bungmati.

have had children. While national literacy stands at an average of 26 percent, only 13 percent of females are literate compared to the male level of 38 percent.

Moving Forward

Nepal is a poor nation for many reasons, but the results of this poverty are clear. Deprived of many basic needs, most of the people experience severe hardship every day, and children are often denied fundamental childhood rights. They deserve better because, like all children, they are the future. Instead of thinking of themselves as victims or people to be pitied, the adults and the children of Nepal are actively working together to improve their own communities. At the same time, the Nepalese government looks for solutions to the country's problems, and international organizations support groups within Nepal to better the lives of all their citizens.

Akka

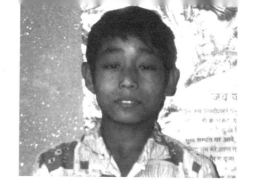

My name is Akka. I am eleven years old. My hut is in a village that is six hours from Kathmandu by bus. I don't have parents. I used to live with my older brother and his wife. They both worked, so it was my duty to look after the children. I looked after the home and took care of the animals, fetched water and cut grass to feed the animals.

I came to Kathmandu with my aunt and started working in a carpet factory. I worked there for five months from six o'clock in the morning until nine at night. When a Rugmark representative came, I asked him if I could leave the factory. He took me to the transit home and then I was transferred to this rehabilitation center. Now I am in class three.

BY
AKKA

Carpets

I always see looms in the carpet
    factory
But I have no ability to weave.
I thought I should go to school
But I never got a chance.
I tried a lot to study
But my master never allowed me to
    do so.

One day, someone from Rugmark
    came.
I was weaving a carpet.
He asked me
My name
And I answered.
He asked me
Whether I wanted to go to school or
    go home
And I answered
I would love to go to school.

Small

Don't undermine the small.
Small are the ones who will be big
    one day.
We all know drops of water make
    an ocean.

Look at the soil containing various
    particles.
This makes the mountain.
But when we look at the huge
    mountains
Who can say
They are made up of such small
    particles.

By joining the small sticks
The nest of a bird is made.
Each movement of a single day makes
    history.

Join the tiny bricks.
You can erect a temple.
But even if there is a small hole
You can never expect the teapot to be
    full.

People who hate small things
Always remain small.
But people who protect small things
Always remain big.

| Zevan | Namaste!

My name is Zevan. I used to roll the carpet wool in the factory. If a small mistake occurred while I was spinning the wool, the owner of the factory would scold me ruthlessly and reduce my monthly salary. Then my aunt taught me how to weave carpets. When I could not understand, she beat me badly.

One day, a man from Rugmark came. He asked me whether I wanted to go home or to school. I answered that I wanted to go to school.

| Ganesh | My name is Ganesh Tamang. I am thirteen years old. I used to work in the carpet industry. I was very badly beaten there. I just could not stand the pain, so after three months I ran away back to my home. Instead of a warm welcome, I got scoldings from my parents and I was forced to return to the factory. I again returned home, because the behavior of the factory owner never changed. My parents then admitted me to the local school, which was very far away. Since I had to walk for two hours each way from my home to school and back, I gave up the idea of attending school and went back to work in the carpet factory. I worked there for two months.

Finally, one day, a Rugmark representative came and took me to a transit home.

| Ritu | Namaste!

My name is Ritu Magar. Hamro Ghar is beautiful because it is surrounded by gardens. It is a three-story building. The door and the windows are made of wood.

Hamro Ghar is home to sixty-four people and is full of enjoyment. Our teachers are like sisters, and they teach us knitting and sewing as well as the usual classes. We all live as a family in Hamro Ghar with mutual understanding and co-operation. Every Friday, we have contests, sing, dance and learn theater arts. Each Saturday, a dance teacher comes to teach us. Also on Saturdays, we watch Nepal television, clean the house and then go to play.

| Sapana | My name is Sapana and I am thirteen years old. I am from a village, but when I was very small, my family moved to Kathmandu. As a result, I know very little about my village.

At the age of nine, I started working in a carpet factory. I worked there for three years. Along with working in the factory, I also had to look after my younger sister and cook for my family.

I used to see lots of boys and girls going to school in the mornings and I always dreamed of attending school. My parents knew about my ambition. They kept promising they would send me to a school, but they never did. Thinking that one day I would go to school, I worked without saying a word. In this way, my life was passing.

One day, while I was sadly weaving a carpet, Rugmark inspectors arrived and asked me if I wanted to study. I quickly answered, "Yes!" They wrote my name on a paper along with the names of some of my friends and then promised they would came back the next day. The next day, we went with them to the transit home. We stayed there for two months and then we moved to a Rugmark rehabilitation center. I stayed there for eleven months and then moved to another center. After nine months of studying there, I came to this center. At last I am now growing taller!

Urmila

My name is Urmila. When I was small, I lived in a village. My mother loved me a lot but my father was irritated by me. He never liked to see me relax, so he kept me working on chores constantly. If my mother protested, she was beaten or scolded.

My mother had always wanted me to study, but my father never agreed. He only made me work and he never cared about feeding me. After whole days of work, I felt very hungry and cried for food. My mother would hide some food and give it to me after my father went to sleep.

Every day, after I washed my face, I went into the jungle in search of firewood. For the whole day I worked on an empty stomach. I only ate in the evening. My father was an alcoholic and he beat my mother every day when he came home.

One morning, my mother and I realized that my father was dead. We cried a lot and then I found out that my mother was pregnant.

The day after my father's death, my mother and I came to Kathmandu. We both started working in a carpet factory. While we learned to weave carpets, my mother and I were often badly beaten and scolded by the master. Sometimes we were not even given anything to eat.

My mother gave birth to a sweet little girl one day. After my sister was born, my mother had to rest so I had to weave the carpets alone. If I stopped, my family would starve. I was so busy working that sometimes I would even forget to eat. The master hated that my mother rested. He thought she was lazy so he kept scolding us.

He told us to leave his place and even threw our clothes out.

We moved to another factory. I worked alone for a month and then my mother and I started working together. In this way, our lives were passing.

One day, some Rugmark inspectors came. One of them asked me, "What do you do here?"

I answered, "I weave carpets." He asked me about my family and talked with my mother for a long time. Afterwards, he took me with him to the Rugmark transit home. I had lots of friends and was very happy. I felt that this was a very good opportunity for me to study and to get a better life. I thought that if I studied, I could be a great person. The school provided food, clothes and study time.

Then I went to a rehabilitation center. I cried a lot when I was moved to that school, but I got a very warm welcome there. I was given new clothes and a lot of fruit. This place was better than the previous one because I could play a lot.

I was very unhappy again when I was moved to another center. But the new place was well managed and beautiful. Right now, I am studying in class six.

When I grow up, I want to be a social worker. I will go to my village to educate people that even girls should go to school. I will talk about how to keep my village clean and I will tell them about how important forests are. This vegetation should not be destroyed in the name of firewood. First I will show them how to practice these habits. Then I will let them live the life themselves.

I believe all the children of the world should be neat and clean because if they do this, they will be healthy. When they are healthy, they can join the fight for children's rights and use these rights to the fullest degree.

The story about my life is really long, but I have only written what I can recall. So I think this is only a small part of my long life. Thank you.

A Poor Man's Daughter

I am a poor man's daughter.
By reading
And writing
I will be a gentle girl.
I will
Develop my country
In the future
By studying well.

I am a poor man's daughter.
Still I respect everyone.
I will
Prove to be good
And not go against
My mother's word.

BY
AKKA

I am a poor man's daughter.
I will
Climb Mount Everest.
In the future
I will
Make my country's name known
By studying hard.

I am a small child
Almost like a bud
Of a flower.
I have to be
A social worker
To uplift many children
Like me.
I will
Not only talk
But prove by performing
That I am
A real social worker.

Aaiti My name is Aaiti and I am fifteen years old. In my village, my father had six children. He was an alcoholic so he never worked. My mother looked after my younger siblings, cooked and worked in the fields. I looked after the cattle and cut the grass.

One day, my father sold everything and took my whole family to Kathmandu to work in the carpet industry. Once I was very sick and my mother asked for money from my master for my treatment. He refused and my mother was forced to borrow money from another person. Unfortunately, she was never able to pay it back.

Eventually, the Rugmark inspectors visited the carpet factory where I was working. My master hid me inside the sleeping quarters. He told me that if I was caught, I had to lie about my true age. The Rugmark representative kept coming, but was never given the correct information.

One day, he approached me and quietly asked about my actual age. I did not give him an honest answer because the master kept warning me. The inspector showed so much love toward me that I decided to tell him the truth. Afterwards, I was scolded badly by the master. He asked me how I thought my family would survive. Since my two elder sisters were fourteen and fifteen, they did not come to the Rugmark school. I came to the transit home with my younger sister who was six years old and had been rolling wool.

I studied at one rehabilitation center for two years and passed class two. Then I came to this center where I learned very quickly. After one year, I am now studying in class six.

In the future, I want to open a tailoring shop. I will teach girls like myself, who are poor or have been rescued from carpet factories, to sew. I think that all children should get an education and have a bright future. Organizations like Rugmark should be open in various parts of the world for children.

| Anil | I came to Kathmandu from my home village to weave carpets. When I was weaving, there was a lot of pressure on my hands and feet. I used to cry thinking about my life. Everyone scolded me, saying, "This boy cries too much!" As a result, I had a very low weaving speed. I never got my food on time or slept well. I had to wake up early in the morning and start to weave without washing my face.

I had a great desire to study. Today, my dream has finally been fulfilled. Now I am studying in class two.

| Kalpana | My name is Kalpana. I am fifteen years old. My home is in a village. My father worked breaking boulders while my mother worked in the house. We owned no fields. There were six children. I had to look after my younger sisters and brothers, cut grass for the cattle, look after the cattle and fetch water.

One of my cousins told me that working in the carpet factory would offer an opportunity for a better life, so I decided to go to work at the age of seven. I was so small then because my growth was stunted from the lack of nutritious food and all the work. The master didn't want me to work on the looms so instead I cooked for him and the workers. I had to wake up the workers at four in the morning and could only go to bed at eleven at night after all my work was finished. I had to wash the master's clothes as well as all the pots, plates and cups.

One day a Rugmark inspector found me and I decided to go with him to the Rugmark transit home. I studied at one rehabilitation center until class two. Then I moved to another center to study higher classes. After being at this Rugmark school for one year, I have just enrolled in class six.

Kailash

Namaste!

My name is Kailash. I am twelve years old. I don't have any parents. I used to work in India as a domestic servant and then was taught how to weave carpets. I came back to Nepal and started to weave carpets in a factory. I worked there for two years, from six in the morning until nine in the evening.

When an inspector came from Rugmark, he explained to the workers and the owner about child rights. After two days, I was taken to the transit home. I stayed there for two weeks and then I was transferred to this rehabilitation center. Now I am happy and am studying in class three.

I believe that all children have basic needs, including food, shelter, clothes, clean air, water suitable to drink and light. Children should be given the time to play, eat and sleep all at appropriate times during the day or night. Children should not be forced to do anything against their will, even by their parents. For example, if a child wants to study, the father shouldn't force her or him to work in the fields all day.

When I grow up, I want to be a medical doctor. There were so many people in my village who died of minor illnesses. I want to treat them and keep my village people healthy.

Hamro Ghar
(Our Home)

We have one small home.
This home is decorated
With windows and doors.
From all directions
How beautiful it looks.

Our small house
Is surrounded by gardens
Including the big and
    the small.
About sixty people
    live here.

Our small house is so
    beautiful.
We get everyone's love
In this small house.
We get an opportunity to
    learn many things
In this small house.

How beautiful is this
Small house of ours.
Though our family is large,
Made up of sixty members,
We are happy and contented
    here.

BY KAILASH

Wake Up!

Wake up!
Encourage yourself to develop
And work.
You have already slept
Far too long
So quit sleeping
And wake up!

Aakash

Namaste!

My name is Aakash. My mother used to work in a carpet factory. I had to stay at home and cook rice for all my family members. For five months we ran into some critical problems and we could not even pay the house rent. One day, while I was in the carpet factory with my mother, a Rugmark representative arrived and, with my mother's permission, took me away from the factory.

When I am older, I want to become a teacher in a village. I have been inspired by the teachers of Hamro Ghar who are so friendly and helpful.

I believe that all the children of the world should have the chance to study. Most of all, every child in the world should have time to play.

BY *Aakash*

Hamro Ghar

This small rehabilitation center
Hamro Ghar.
We stay here.
We read, write
And do our work here.

We are small children.
Our duty is to study now.
We learn many things
In our Hamro Ghar.

We peep in and out
And play hide and seek.

We run here and there.
Sometimes we read
Or write
Or play.

We always stay here.
We seek knowledge
and do our work.
Learning good things
Here we will become
Good people in the
Future.

27

Kanta

Namaste!

My name is Kanta. I am twelve years old. I used to work in the carpet industry. There I had to face a lot of difficulties. I lived in the factory, where I had to work very hard. I used to weave carpets from five o'clock in the morning until ten o'clock at night. Once I had finished my work, it was my dinner time. Then I could go to bed. The next morning I woke up and followed the same old routine. In this way, my life passed slowly because I had no desire or interest to work.

One day, a representative from Rugmark visited our factory and asked me if I would like to study. I answered yes, but said that I was afraid of what my master would do. After the man convinced my master to let me leave, he explained to me that I was not to worry because he had settled everything. I agreed without a complaint. A couple of days later, he came to rescue me and I happily went with him to the transit home. After studying there for quite some time, I moved to a rehabilitation center called BABK. I am very happy here and I have to face no such troubles as I had to in the carpet industry.

When I grow up, I would like to be a dancer so that I can collect funds to improve and build more rehabilitation centers for working children.

I believe that no children in the world should experience unhappiness. They should all have the opportunity to study in a school like BABK, where they can be taught in a friendly atmosphere.

| Sumitra | My name is Sumitra. I'm thirteen years old. In my village, I was responsible for all of the household chores.

My father used to beat me and yell at me to leave the house. I hid in the bushes at night. The next day, my family members would come and insist that I return home. As I played hide and seek with my family, my life was passing. Yet I was happy enough because I knew that underneath, my parents loved me.

One day, my uncle and my aunt came from Kathmandu. They promised my family that they would take me to the city to be educated. So I went to Kathmandu. However, instead of attending school, I started to work at a carpet factory. My uncle and aunt were very rude. They never let me go home and I was often scolded and beaten. They took all the money I earned. Every day, I would remember my parents and cry.

The next year, during the holiday of Dashain, I was able to go home. When I returned to Kathmandu, a Rugmark inspector found me.

| Youmaya | My name is Youmaya. When I was three months old, my father married another woman and left us. My mother, brother and I went to India to look for jobs. We came back to Nepal when I was three years old. My mother worked in the fields and my brother looked after the cattle. Eventually, we could no longer afford the land and had to stop working. Then no one in my family was earning money, so my brother joined the army. I was four or five years old and I went to work in a hospital canteen. My brother had to go and fight, but he was afraid of wars. My mother insisted that he go because he was the only source of a real income. My father had worked in the army and my mother insisted that his life had been good. But my brother returned from the war with terribly injured hands. A bullet had ripped open a hole in his hand. However, he still went to work in a carpet factory in Kathmandu.

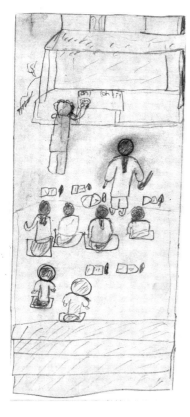

I went with him to the city. At first my brother made me work in a hotel, and he took my salary. I don't even know how much I earned. Then I started working in a carpet factory. By then my brother was married.

One day, a Rugmark inspector came. Although my sister-in-law didn't think girls should go to school, my brother gave me permission to leave. Now I am at a Rugmark rehabilitation center and am studying in class six.

Balbadhur

My name is Balbadhur. I believe that the children of the world should never have to suffer from poverty. They should have the chance to study as I have had at this center. Right now, I am fourteen years old and would like to be trained as a Rugmark inspector. Then I can bring children to a transit home and help them learn to read.

Raju

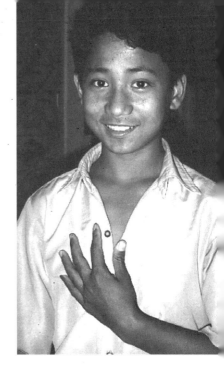

My name is Raju. I am fourteen years old. I was born in Kathmandu. My parents worked in a carpet factory. I went to study in a school at the age of four. After I finished class four, my parents did not think I should go to school. I started working in a carpet factory.

At first I rolled the wool. Then I learned to weave carpets. It took me two months to learn how to weave. Then, one day, I told my mother that I wanted to continue my education. She told me that I first had to earn some money and then she would send me to school.

After that, I would remind my mother of her agreement to send me to school, but she insisted that I earn money. I was tired of arguing with her, so I decided to forget about studying. Even I started to be willing to earn money instead of going to school.

In the days that passed, my mind was only concerned with earning money. I got up at five o'clock in the morning and worked until eleven o'clock at night. During the festival times, I worked through the night.

One day, my younger brother and I had just finished eating when we met a Rugmark representative. He asked several questions and then he asked if I wanted to study. I could not answer because I knew there was an economic problem in my home. The Rugmark representative told me that I could go with him, but first he wanted to consult with my parents. My parents refused to let

me go because my father thought that my brother and I had to earn money since he was aging.

After a very long discussion, the Rugmark representative was able to convince my parents, and I was taken to the transit home with my brother. That's where I learned what the Rugmark Foundation was. I was transferred to one rehabilitation center before coming to this one. I studied in class five. After passing that, I was moved into class seven. Now I am in class eight.

Here I have learned many things. I have become big and have learned the differences between right and wrong. I want to thank the Rugmark Foundation a trillion times for lighting children's shadowy lives. I also want to thank Tanya Didi for letting me write my story.

When I grow up, I want to be a doctor because there are few health posts in villages. A lot of my cousins and friends have died from simple diseases.

My message to villagers is that it is not wise to come to Kathmandu in search of money. A young friend of mine from a village began working in a carpet factory and almost died from being beaten by his master.

I believe parents should be every child's role models. All children should play very little and instead study. They should try to participate in all school programs and in national and international activities if possible. They should never hesitate and should always keep trying.

Parwati

My name is Parwati. In the village where I lived until I was nine years old, I got up at five o'clock. After washing my face, I would go and get the grass for the cattle. Then I had dhero and went into the jungle to cut branches for firewood. After returning from there, I didn't have a single minute to rest. I washed the pots, plates and cups as well as the clothes.

While my father worked in Kathmandu, my mother worked in other people's fields from early in the morning. My brothers and sisters were very small so I had to clean the house, make the beds and cook tiffin (afternoon meal) for my siblings. I never had any of this food because there was not enough. During the day, my siblings would sleep. I would bring unrefined wool from a storage outlet and spin and braid the wool so that it could be sent to a carpet factory. In the evening, I cooked rice and curry for my family. My mother returned home late in the evening. Once she was home, I served food to my family. After my mother, who was very weak, and my siblings had gone to sleep, I washed the dishes and then I worked on the wool. I was able to go to sleep at 11:30. At this time, I was only five or six years old.

When I was nine, I was taken to a carpet factory by one of my neighbors who had promised to educate me. I don't know where my neighbor went, but I never saw him after I started working. I woke up at five and worked until nine at night. I only had time for two meals during the day. I never received any wages. Instead, I was allowed to eat and sleep there. I slept on the floor in the carpet

My Life BY *Parwati*

My life
Is a flowing river.
I spend
My lonely life
In sorrow.
All people
Discriminate against me
Because I am poor.
I think
It is better
To die than
To live.
My life
Is deserted and
Filled with tears.

factory. The toilet was a hole and had walls made of sacks, but the master had a real toilet.

When I was weaving the carpets, there was a lot of dust. Due to this dust, I had the first stages of tuberculosis. Since I was sick, I stopped working on the carpets. But instead of resting, I cooked for the master and his family and washed their clothes and all the cooking utensils. If the food didn't taste perfect, I would be scolded and beaten. I worked at this factory for two years.

When I grow up, I want to become a doctor so I can make sure children who are poor like myself are healthy without charging them a fee. No matter how poor children might be, they should not tell everyone that they are poor. Instead, they should be determined to find a way to honestly earn their living.

Urmila

Namaste!

My name is Urmila. I am twelve years old. When I was nine years old, I had to face many problems. My parents went to Kathmandu and my aunt was given the responsibility of taking care of me. Instead of loving me, she made me do all the housework, like looking after her baby and the animals. If I made a small mistake, she treated me badly.

I began to work in a carpet factory with her in Kathmandu. I had to look after my aunt's child and cook the food when we got home. My aunt never helped me with my household chores.

One day, my mother came. She had earned some money and now she was working in another carpet factory. Her salary was 2000 rupees a month (about $42 CAN, $27 U.S.). She asked me if I wanted to attend school. However, I realized that Rs 2000 would hardly be enough to buy food for the family and pay the room rent. My father was an alcoholic and did not work.

I asked my mother to try to get me a job on the same loom as her. My mother's master agreed, but my salary was very low. Once I was suffering from diarrhea, but I had to continue working because my master thought that diarrhea was not a sickness.

One day, a Rugmark representative arrived and convinced my

master and my mother that I should not have to work. I decided to go with him. That's how I came to a Rugmark school.

When I grow up, I want to help exploited child workers. Whatever I have learned, I will share with them. I would like to set up a rehabilitation center for them. Then, together, we can show the world that these children can learn and become great people.

I believe that all children should have the chance to study. The children who do not have this opportunity need to be supported by organizations like Rugmark. Then all of these children can become great people who are friendly, helpful and do not discriminate against anyone in any way.

Rambhadur

Namaste!

My name is Rambhadur. I used to work in a carpet factory. One day, a Rugmark representative came and told me about the Rugmark school. At that time, I didn't know what school was. I was afraid to go, but the Rugmark person explained it in such detail that I realized I really did want to go.

I was first taken to the transit home, but I felt very inferior. Even though I spoke Nepali, I didn't know ka, kha, ga. Other children knew this alphabet already, but I didn't. Then I was taken to a rehabilitation center where I learned to write a few words. Later I was brought to this Rugmark school.

When I first arrived, I was very unhappy. I had no friends and the surroundings were unfamiliar. After a few days, I made many friends and I became very happy. Now, seeing my friends and teachers every day makes me smile.

Threat

I would like to climb a tree
But I am afraid
Of falling down.

I would like to eat a mango
But I am afraid
Of the diarrhea.

I would like to see a tiger
But I am afraid
That the tiger will eat me.

I would like to fight
But I am afraid
Of the wounds.

I would like to ride in a car
But I am afraid
Of the accident.

I would like to play outside
But I am afraid
Of losing.

BY RAMBHADUR

Ram Kumar

My name is Ram Kumar. I am fifteen years old. When I was five, my two sisters, my elder brother and my father went to work in a carpet factory, so I ended up doing all the work.

I used to wake up at four o'clock in the morning. My mother would take the goats to the jungle and bring back grass for the cattle. I looked after the cattle and sold buffalo milk in the local dairy. After coming back from the dairy, I cooked food for my younger brother and fed him. Then I would clean the cattle and the cattle shed. After that, I would go to the field to fetch some vegetables to cook curry and dhero. Then my mother would come and we would eat together.

Afterwards, I would walk for two hours to a faraway hillside to collect firewood and green branches for the cattle to sleep on. One day, while I was doing this, I accidentally cut off part of my finger.

When I came back from the hillside, my mother prepared food for me. After we ate, it would be about nine o'clock, so we went to sleep.

When I was ten years old, my older sister returned to our village and took me to Kathmandu to work in a carpet factory. She was my master, so I was not beaten. I wove carpets, washed her clothes and cooked food for us both. After two years, I was taken to the Rugmark transit home.

I was not happy at the transit home. I didn't know anybody there. After one week, I was transferred to a rehabilitation center where I studied up to class three. I cried a lot at this school because

I didn't know anybody. After four days of feeling sad, I began to become adjusted. I was upset to leave, but I had finished all the classes that were offered there. Then I moved to this rehabilitation center to continue my studying. I did so well in class five that after I finished that class, I moved into class seven. In class seven, I graduated at the top of the class. Last year, I received training to be a plumber. Now I am looking for work in Kathmandu.

Since I am poor, I decided that I should become a plumber. If I could continue studying, I would become a doctor. In my village I watched so many people die because the medical posts are far away and there is no medicine available.

I believe that all the children of the world should learn to be independent, because life has no guarantees. They should use all of the opportunities available to them and should learn to be self-dependent.

Samita

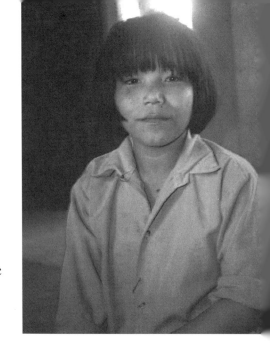

Namaste!

My name is Samita. I am ten years old. When I lived in a village, I had to fetch water from the well each day. One day my bucket fell into the water. My mother scolded me very badly.

I never got good food in my home. We usually had dhero, but eating rice was almost a dream. Looking after the household and the animals was difficult.

While I looked after the animals in the field, I used to play with bhadakuti. One day I was so absorbed in my game that the animals wandered off into another field. My mother scolded me so badly that I started to wonder why I had the misfortune of being born female.

Eventually my family managed to acquire some rice. I wanted to try to cook it but I didn't cook it very well. All the members of my family, including my father, scolded me so much.

When I grow up, I would like to be a social worker for children.

I believe that every family should have fewer children so that each one can have sufficient food, clothes and education. No matter how much children may have, there should always be big smiles on their faces so they can have the strength to carry out their lives. All children should have a bright future so that they can grow up and be employed in professions to help others.

The children of all the different countries must unite to make this world a better place.

Suresh

When I was seven, my mother wove carpets and my father worked in the factory helping out in the management. I have two younger sisters and one younger brother. At that time I could not study.

One day, my father abandoned my family. We had nowhere to go because my father would not keep my mother at his home anymore. So my mother kept all of us children at her brother's home. Her brother was very poor and had a large family, but he allowed us to live with him. Since there were so many people in this home, there was only enough food to eat once a day.

Once the crops did not grow in my uncle's field. My uncle took a loan from an agriculture bank and even now he is still unable to repay that debt. I studied up to class three in a school nearby without paying money, but I could only write A, B, C and ka, kha, ga. Then I left school and started to work. I used to wake up at four o'clock in the morning and cut and bring the grass for the cattle. Then I walked for three hours to take the cattle to graze in the jungle.

Later I went with my mother and uncle to Kathmandu to learn to weave carpets. My uncle and mother decided that they could begin to pay off his debt with the money I earned.

One day a Rugmark representative came to the factory where I was weaving. He asked me if I wanted to study. I answered yes. He asked me why I wove carpets. At that time, I wished that he had experienced a condition like mine so that he would have known my problems. After a pause, I answered that I needed to earn a liv-

ing and pay off my uncle's debt. Then he took me to the transit home.

I learned A, B, C, which I had already forgotten. I stayed there for three months. Then I was transferred to a rehabilitation center. I attended class three. I learned many things, like discipline, how to adjust, and to make friends. I also learned that one should never be envious or steal. One must be satisfied with what one has. Since there was no class four at this center, I was transferred to another center. Right now, I'm in class five.

I am studying with an aim to become a doctor. I'm very grateful to the Rugmark staff that I am able to enjoy a happy life now. But I'm worried about the many children who are spoiling their lives by playing cards and stealing so they can buy more cards. They are making a lot of trouble for their families. In my uncle's village, they tried to convince me that I should play cards with them. I told them it was a bad habit and that they should all be studying. Some of them answered that their parents were very poor and couldn't educate them.

I wished that I could bring these friends here. So I promised them I would try to find a way for them to go to school. I have never been able to speak to anyone about my friends. That's why I'm writing this message through this letter. If you really want to help, and you can, then please find a way to educate my friends. They are the future of Nepal. It is my polite request that these children be educated so that they can become great citizens of the world.

Working Together
to Make Dreams a Reality

Rugmark was transformed from an idea into an international trademark in 1994, when consumers in Germany pressured stores to carry hand-woven carpets made without child labor. Human rights groups in Germany and India helped draw attention to the issue. Soon, carpet exporters in India and importers in Germany saw their sales fall as a result of the publicity, and some companies agreed to implement the Rugmark criteria to improve working conditions in their factories and eliminate child labor. Today, more than thirty percent of the carpets sold in Germany bear the Rugmark label.

As consumers, we can bring about change. Every time we buy something — whether it is shoes, soccer balls or clothes — we have the power to pressure companies and governments to respect children's and workers' rights. Ask the staff at your favorite store whether they can stock their shelves with products that have labels certifying that the workers who made the clothes or harvested the food were paid properly, were not abused and were not children who were being exploited. Write letters to store managers and tell them that you want the products you buy to be made under fair labor conditions. Already, fair trade labels on food and clothing are becoming accepted in countries such as the Netherlands, Australia, the United Kingdom, Canada and the United States. But it is up to us to pressure companies to carry merchandise bearing these labels.

Labeling imports is not the whole solution. It will not bring an end to the most harmful forms of child labor. That is because chil-

Students of the Co-operative Society of Bungmati.

dren and exploited workers are employed in many industries – for example in mines, in cigarette factories, as rag pickers and in brothels. When responding to the problem of child labor, many other issues need to be addressed, such as low wages, sexism, expensive school fees and poverty. International and local groups need to work together. Organizations such as Rugmark, the Ethical Trading Initiative and TransFair collaborate with citizens' movements such as the South Asian Coalition on Child Servitude, Women Working Worldwide and Students Against Sweatshops. Together, these groups are working toward a time when everyone has access to the rights that we take for granted, such as clean water, sufficient food, education, health care, shelter and dignity. Granting all workers the right to form independent trade unions is another key part of a long-term solution, because unions can more effectively demand improvements in wages and working conditions.

Today it is often students who are coming up with creative ways to inform the public about the problems of child labor and what we can do about it. They are putting on dramas, anti-sweatshop fashion shows and street parties to make their points.

Young people need to work together to understand and help each other. You, too, can make a difference. Whether you are nine or nineteen years old, you can help to bring about the day when every child's basic needs and rights are met.

Resources

Websites may change without notice. At press time, all sites listed here were in full operation.
• Rugmark International **http://www.rugmark.de/english/**, Rugmark U.S.A. **http://www.rugmark.org** and Rugmark Nepal **http://www.nepalrugmark.org** have Websites with information on Rugmark schools and programs. Rugmark U.S.A. has a special site developed for young people.

Other Organizations and Websites:
• American Federation of Teachers – Child Labor Project **http://www.aft.org/international/child/** provides instructional materials and an information package.
• Child Workers in Nepal Concerned Centre (CWIN) **http://www.cwin-nepal.org/** is one of the main advocate organizations in Nepal working to promote children's rights and to eliminate exploitative child labor. This colorful but serious site describes the situation of child rights in Nepal, features specific issues and has a photo archive, details of programs, on-line publications and press releases. Listserv available.
• Free the Children **http://www.freethechildren.com/** is an international network of children helping children through representation, leadership and action. Advocates for the elimination of child labor and the provision of universal primary education. Campaigns, resources and projects for young people.
• International Labour Organization Child Labour Site **http://www.ilo.org/public/english/comp/child/** includes documents, policies

and conventions pertaining to child labor. The ILO also has a Virtual Classroom on Child Labour **http://us.ilo.org/ilokidsnew/index.html** with resources and activities for students at all grade levels.
• The Kids Campaign to Build a School for Iqbal **http://mirrorimage.com/iqbal/index.html** was founded by a group of middle school students. The campaign raises money to support schools in Pakistan in honor of Iqbal Masih, a former child carpet weaver and activist. Photographs from schools in Pakistan, action ideas and updates.
• Maquila Solidarity Network **http://www.maquilasolidarity.org/resources/child/index.htm** promotes solidarity with workers' groups in free trade zones to support their struggles for better employment conditions and fair wages. The Child Labour Resource Site features articles and links providing an overall perspective of child labor as part of the struggle for just working conditions for all. Includes an issue paper with a section by Tanya Roberts-Davis.
• One World Guide on Child Labour **http://www.oneworld.org/guides/chld_labour/index.html** is informative but brief, with excellent links and news items.
• UNICEF Child Labor Site **http://www.unicef.org/aclabor** offers an interactive quiz and conference papers, with a focus on child domestic servants.
• UNICEF Voices of Youth Site **http://www.unicef.org/voy** provides online discussions, archives and activities on global issues concerning youth.

The following Websites deal specifically with fair trade issues:
• Fair TradeMark Canada **http://www.transfair.ca/who/fair2.htm**; Labour Behind the Label Campaign (UK) **http://www.cleanclothes.org/codes/inilivingwa.htm**; Transfair USA **http://www.transfairusa.org**; Students Against Sweatshops – Canada **http://www.campuslife.utoronto.ca/groups/opirg/groups/sweatshops/sas-c.html**; United Students Against Sweatshops **http://www.usasnet.org**.

Videos
• *Rights and Wrongs: Child Labor*, Global Vision, 1995. A 30-minute film about child bondage in the Pakistan carpet industry. Contact the Global Center (ref: Child Labor#305), Tel: 212-246-0202.
• *Shackled Children*, International Labour Organization, 1993. A 55-minute film about child carpet weavers in India, children working in jasmine harvesting and leather tanning in Egypt, young migrant workers in the U.S. and child miners in Colombia. Contact the International Labour Organization, Tel: 202-653-7652.

Publications
• *Challenging Child Labour* by the Canadian Labour Congress, 1998. Contact the International Department, CLC, 2841 Riverside Drive, Ottawa, ON K1V 8X7.
• "Child Labor: Our Lives, Our Words," Special Issue, *The New Internationalist*, No. 293, July 1997. *New Internationalist*, 35 Riviera Dr., Unit 17, Markham L3R 8N4 Canada. Features first-hand stories

and opinions by working children, unforeseen consequences of boycotts, a historical perspective and overall analyses of the situation now.
• *Listen to Us! The World's Working Children* by Jane Springer, Groundwood Books, 1997. Explores the complexities of child labor with personal stories, photographs and charts. For ages 12 and up.
• *Free the Children: A Young Man's Personal Crusade Against Child Labor* by Craig Kielburger and Kevin Major, Harper Collins,1999. How twelve-year-old Kielburger responded to the issue of exploitative child labor by forming the youth organization Free the Children. For ages 12 and up.
• *Iqbal Masih and the Crusaders Against Child Slavery* by Susan Kuklin, Henry Holt, 1998. Describes the life of Iqbal, a bonded carpet weaver killed at the age of twelve because of his outspoken activism against child labor; how students in the U.S. continued Iqbal's struggle. For ages 12 and up.

Glossary

bhadakuti – toy kitchen utensils made out of aluminum or plastic

caste system – in ancient times, the Hindu division of people based on occupations; in modern times, a hereditary social ranking system

constitution – the written rules and laws by which a country is governed

consumer – someone who purchases and uses items such as food and clothing

Dashain – the largest annual festival in Nepal, taking place in September/October over the course of ten days

debt bondage – a form of modern slavery in which a person works without any wages in order to pay off a debt

democracy – a form of government that is influenced by a substantial part of the population through direct participation or the election of representatives

dhero – dough made from corn flour

fodder – food for livestock that is made out of dried grasses

Hamro Ghar – Nepali phrase meaning "our home"; an informal name for BABK, a Rugmark rehabilitation center

ka, kha, ga – the first three letters of the Nepali alphabet

Kathmandu – the capital city of Nepal

literacy – the ability to read and write

monsoon – a wind that brings unusually heavy rains in summer

namaste – the Nepali greeting meaning both hello and goodbye

Rugmark – a labeling initiative that certifies carpets from India, Nepal and Pakistan have only been made by adults paid at least the legal minimum wage

Rugmark rehabilitation center – a place for former child carpet weavers to receive counseling, health care and an education

Rugmark transit home – the center to which children are brought after they leave the carpet factory, where they are given intense care and are assessed so that they can be placed in an appropriate rehabilitation center

rupee – the currency used in Nepal; US$1.00 = Rs74 / CAN$1.00 = Rs48

sexism – the unfair treatment of a person based on whether he or she is male or female

squatter – a person who settles on land that he or she does not own

sweatshop – a workplace where employees work under poor and unfair conditions and do not have the right to organize a union

textiles – fabrics made by knitting, weaving or sewing

tiffin – a small mid-day meal

trade union – an association of workers organized to deal with an employer collectively to demand that their rights are respected

tuberculosis – an infectious disease of the lungs

UNICEF – the United Nations Children's Fund, which advocates the protection of children's rights through programs and the funding of projects around the world

United Nations Convention on the Rights of the Child – an international human rights treaty that covers children's legal, civil and social rights